Backc

MW01025727

Doug Gilmer - The Backcountry Chaplain

Published by Backcountry Adventures Press

Cover photo by James Overstreet

Copyright 2012 Doug Gilmer

Scripture References

Scripture quotations marked ESV are taken from The Holy Bible, English Standard Version® (ESV®), copyright © 2001, 2011 by Crossway Bibles, a publishing ministry of Good News Publishers. Used by permission. All rights reserved.

Scripture quotations marked NIV are taken from The Holy Bible, New International Version® NIV® Copyright © 1973, 1984, 2011 by Biblica, Inc. ™

Scripture quotations marked NKJV are taken from the New King James Version. Copyright © 1982 by Thomas Nelson, Inc. Used by permission.

The Backcountry Chaplain™ and "Leading Lives Lived Outside"™ are trademarks belonging to Douglas Gilmer.

www.BackcountryAdventurePress.com

Backcountry Devotions

Volume 1

Table Of Contents

4

Acknowledgements

There are far too many people I must acknowledge in the writing of this book. I am sure to miss someone I should list so I apologize in advance.

Thank you to Tron and Misty Peterson for your encouragement and urging me to put these devotions in a book. Thank you too for your friendship and all you do to support our service members.

Thank you to my friend, Rabbi Jamie Korngold, aka The Adventure Rabbi. Although we may differ theologically and philosophically in some regards, your friendship and wisdom motivate me and I am thankful for the creative ways you taught me to see God in the Wilderness.

Thank you Dave Hentosh; because every man needs a best friend.

Thank you David Blanton and for your help in creating The Backcountry Chaplain.

Thank you to all of my friends and Twitter followers. Without you, your support, your re-tweets, comments, and support, this would not have been possible.

And thank you to my publisher Darin Letzring for reading the BackcountryChaplain.com and believing this could in fact be a book.

Dedication

This book is dedicated to my amazing family; Pam, Hayden, Holden, and Kaylie. Thanks for sticking by me, believing in me, and for the privilege of sharing life with each of you.

To my parents, my brothers, and my sister for encouraging me and allowing me to pursue my outdoor passions when I was young.

To Dr. Elmer Towns, whose words to me 25 years ago still motivate me today, "If you want to reach the world, reach for the pen."

To my Adventure Leadership & Outdoor Ministry students at Liberty University, past and present, you are the best!

It is not the length of life, but the depth.

- Ralph Waldo Emerson

Fourteen Seconds...

"And just as it is appointed for man to die once, and after that comes judgment," Hebrews 9:27 ESV

Right now, stop what you are doing. Clear your head, cut out any distractions and look at your watch. Count as 14 seconds ticks by. It feels longer than we assume.

Recently a story in the news made me pause and seriously contemplate my life. A well-known and respected Ranger with the National Park Service, an expert climber and mountain rescue specialist, was called up to rescue a group of climbers who had become trapped on Mt. Rainier. The ranger selflessly answered the call to duty to do the job he was trained and sworn to do. After rescuing most of the helpless individuals, however, something happened. We don't know what happened, but something went tragically wrong. According to the reports, this highly skilled, highly trained rescuer somehow became detached from his lines and fell 3000 feet to his death.

As one who has spent 25 years in the public safety profession, not to mention a career in the Coast Guard, I related to this story on personal level. Any time another public servant dies in the line of duty it bothers me. Yet what really struck me was the fact he fell 3000 feet. Some quick math showed it would take about 14 seconds to fall that distance. I have to wonder what one thinks about when they realize in 14 seconds their life is going to end and there is nothing they can do to stop it. Are there thoughts about what should have, could have, and what might have been? Are there regrets? Are there thoughts about eternity and what is next at the end of the 14 seconds?

We don't like to think much about the end of our lives, the "after this" of Hebrews 9:27. Yet, it's a certainty for all of us and none of us knows when. No matter how well equipped, trained, or respected we may be, we are going to all die eventually, after this, we will be judged. I think the reason we are so disturbed by these words and don't really like to think about the "after this" is summed up in the fact that the extent and depth of our sin is really known only by you and God. The idea off being held accountable after we die scares us. Yet we all will be.

The words "after this" should cause us to stop and seriously examine our lives just as knowing we suddenly only had 14 more seconds to live. John 3:16-17 is an incredible promise, "For God so loved the world, that he gave his only Son, that whoever believes in him should not perish but have eternal life." God's will for you is that you accept the free gift of eternal life that is offered to you, paid for by Jesus' death on the cross. The blood he shed that day covered the sins of the world, past, present, and future, and ushered in an age of grace whereby anyone, regardless of status or past, can be saved. Romans 10:9-10 tells us how it's done, "because, if you confess with your mouth that Jesus is Lord and believe in your heart that God raised him from the dead, you will be saved. For with the heart one believes and is justified, and with the mouth one confesses and is saved." There is no amount of good you can do without Jesus to save you but there is no amount of bad you can do with his forgiveness that can keep you out.

"After this" could be the two of the most dreaded words in the entire Bible. No one wants to dwell on death. However, if you have placed your faith and trust in Jesus Christ and acknowledged the forgiveness he offers, there is no reason to fear the judgment. For those who have, "after this" is simply a new beginning to an amazing eternity spent in fellowship with God.

For those who have not, an eternity is spent separated from God in a place called hell.

Now look at your watch and count those same 14 seconds again. As you do, pretend you only have those 14 seconds left to live and think about this; what do you need to do in these last seconds to prepare for the "after this."

Life is either a daring adventure - or nothing.

– Helen Keller

Not all who wander are lost.

— J.R.R. Tolkien

Wilderness

Remember how the Lord your God led you all the way in the wilderness these forty years, to humble and test you in order to know what was in your heart, whether or not you would keep his commands. Deuteronomy 8:2 NIV

Did you know that term "wilderness" has a legal definition? The Wilderness Act of 1964 defined what wilderness is from a legal perspective rather than just the dictionary's literary definition. In part, the Wilderness Act says wilderness is characterized as a place where "earth and its community of life are untrammeled by man, where man himself is a visitor who does not remain". It adds, the wilderness is a place without permanent improvements or habitation by man, is at least 5000 acres, has some intrinsic value, where man's influence is unnoticeable, where it maintains its "primeval character", and possesses outstanding opportunities "for solitude" and unconfined recreation. Sounds great! But remember, according to the definition, it is a great place to visit, but you can't live there.

Sometimes we go to the wilderness by choice. It is after all, a great place for recreation, relaxation, and reflection. It is a great escape as you are finally free from the distractions of daily life and man's influence. However, to go to the wilderness unwillingly and unprepared could be a very formidable and frightening experience. To be suddenly left stranded and forced to survive would not be on anyone "must do" list, unless of course you have your own TV survivor show.

Sometimes our trip to the wilderness, at least a figurative one, is not by choice. Sometimes in life we go through periods of life and experience in which we feel alone, neglected, and it is all we can do to just survive. It might feel as if the world has turned against you, each day it seems you face new trials, and around every turn you are being tested once again. Maybe you really are being tested.

In Deuteronomy 8:2, God's chosen people, are reminded how they were allowed to roam the wilderness for 40 years all because God wanted to test their character to see if they were worthy of what he planned for them. You see, God had an incredible plan in store for his people, one including a magnificent outcome. Yet, God first wanted to make sure they were up for the task and worthy of the reward. Spending 40 years in the wilderness can build a lot of character.

As difficult as it might seem, maybe your trip through the wilderness (though I seriously doubt it will last 40 years) is meant to test you, to build your character, in preparation for something great God has in store for you down the road. Keeping your current situation in perspective, remaining faithful and pushing through will get you there. If you are in wilderness, figurative or literal, and you give up hope, give up trying to find your way out and just sit down and quit, that is where you will die.

When you find yourself in the wilderness, don't lose hope, it is only temporary. Remain faithful, and focus on the outcome God wants to deliver to you if you remain faithful. You weren't meant to stay in the wilderness and God doesn't want to keep you there. He has bigger plans for you. Even the Wilderness Act says the "wilderness" can be a great place to visit, but you can't live there. Sure, you can choose to die there, but you can't live there. The choice is yours.

When it is dark enough, you can see the stars.
— Ralph Waldo Emerson

Suffering Sucks

I consider that our present sufferings are not worth comparing with the glory that will be revealed in us. Romans 8:18 NIV

Suffering sucks. There is no sense in sugar-coating it or trying to put a good spin on it. No one likes to suffer. The reality is, however, suffering is a reality. No way around it. We are all going to face times in our lives when the pain of suffering from some life experience is going to feel overwhelming. Since we cannot ignore it and pretend it will never happen, we must then determine to understand it.

This verse reveals to us a few of things. First, suffering is temporary. The verse mentions the sufferings of this "present time". This means suffering isn't forever, just for now. It may come in seasons and there may be more than one season of suffering in your life but they are all temporary.

Second, we are promised glory will follow suffering. It isn't the other way around. After all, how miserable would life be if, in the end, we had nothing to look forward to except an eternity of suffering? How terrible would it be if life started out wonderfully only to know if would end horribly. We, however, are promised a future, permanent glory in response to our present, temporary suffering.

Third, the magnitude of our suffering now is not even "worth comparing" to the magnitude of the glory we are promised. A glory made not at the hands of men but by the hand of God and delivered in eternity to those who choose to put their faith and trust in Him. I love the promise we are given in 2 Corinthians 4:16-18,

Therefore we do not lose heart. Though outwardly we are wasting away, yet inwardly we are being renewed day by day. For our light and momentary troubles are achieving for us an eternal glory that far outweighs them all. So we fix our eyes not on what is seen, but on what is unseen, since what is seen is temporary, but what is unseen is eternal.

This brings us to number four. The verse tells us the glory _will be_ revealed to us. It hasn't yet. We may not be able to see it from where we stand right now. Our present suffering may even cloud our understanding of this promise and we may question our faith and ask God "Why?" but it is still a promise. One day, it will be revealed.

The lessons from this verse are something I try and teach students while undertaking outdoor adventure and endurance type activities. Of course I don't try and intentionally make anyone suffer but spending any length of time in the outdoors for some is uncomfortable at best. Extend that time to a few days and you create an environment in which many participants often reach a breaking point. When you finally make the final turn at the trail and re-emerge back into civilization the recent discomforts pale in comparison to the glory they know they are going to soon feel with a hot shower, a meal that is not prepackaged, and of course, Internet service. The students with the right attitude focus on the glory that awaits them.

Suffering is for a season, but also for a reason. It teaches us something. C.S. Lewis once said, "God whispers in our pleasures, speaks in our conscience, but shouts in our pain." How true that is. And just like the future glory we cannot see now, the reason for our suffering may not be clearly seen either. However, in my experience, it is the reason we suffer, which once understood, is what often helps push back the clouds and gives us a glimpse of the glory that awaits us.

No matter what you are going through now or may go through in the future please understand this, suffering sucks, but it's only for now. Glory awaits.

I love to think of nature as having unlimited broadcasting stations, through which God speaks to us every day, every hour and every moment of our lives, if we will only tune in and remain so.

—George Washington Carver

Se~~e~~

Lord, the God of Israel,
earth below – you who
who continue wholehe~~arted~~

Have you ever tri~~ed~~
else? Or maybe
mountain you a~~t~~
right words. It'~~s~~
others were th~~e~~
of what you
describe the ~~
had to be there".

[rotated text along torn edge:] understood it was temporary an~~d~~ God. Next we learn God keeps ~~h~~ your covenant..." Sadl~~y~~ today and it is becom~~ seems we have no integrity is relativ~~ believe will be~~ of promises ~~ the promis~~ promises~~ still k~~ Fi~~

As far as the attributes of God are co~~ncerned~~
be one of the best at describing just how goo~~d~~
people who walk before Him with "wholehearted dev~~otion~~
Solomon's description of God's character is so personal it paints
an amazing picture of his character and what it means to us.

First it teaches us of God's unique nature. There is no other God
"in all of heaven above or on the earth below." The people of the
day had an established track record of building idols and
attempting to follow false gods throughout their history. Of
course each time this ended in catastrophe. Each time, it was God,
THE God, who would step in and ultimately rescue them. God
did some pretty incredible things back then to show His people
that he was the one true God. As for Solomon, he was wealthiest
king who ever lived and even today his wealth would be
considered immense. There was nothing he lacked on earth;
nothing he could not get. Yet despite his wealth, even he as king

d could never take the place of

s promises. Solomon says, "You keep
, a person's word does not mean much
ng harder and harder to trust anyone. It
problem saying "patience is a virtue" but
. People today will often say and do what they
efit them most. Not so with God. The Bible is full
od made and he has kept them all. The best part is
es made by God then, are God's promises now. The
God makes in the Bible are still applicable today and he
eps his word. You can trust God.

ally God's love is unconditional. Solomon experienced this too
and to me, at least, this is God's greatest attribute. God loves us in
spite of ourselves. Despite our sin and the many ways we fail, his
love remains "unfailing". It doesn't matter who you are or what
you have done, God's love toward us remains unchanged. It is not
a cheap love or a love that seeks only to gain favor. It is a love that
is unfailing, uncompromising, unmatched, unconditional, and is
indefinable by human standards. Man has corrupted "love" in so
many different ways and has diminished its meaning. With
divorce rates hovering at 50%, love "til death do us part" has
instead become disposable and matter of convenience. Not so
with God, he never divorces those he loves.

Solomon's picture of God is pretty incredible. Obviously we can
read about just how amazing God is in today's verse. Better yet,
even though we were not there when this was written, God hasn't
changed. As a matter of God is still here; and should you choose,
you can experience Him for yourself.

It's an Adventure!

By faith Abraham, when called to go to a place he would later receive as his inheritance, obeyed and went, even though he did not know where he was going. Hebrews 11:8 NIV

Where is God asking you to go?

An adventure is any experience with an uncertain outcome. This can pretty much sum up Abraham's experience. As you read the account of Abraham in the Old Testament (Genesis 11 & 12) you notice that he was pretty content and comfortable. He had wealth and prestige and everything was going pretty much status quo for him until God showed up and asked him to move outside his comfort zone and begin a true adventure. God promised Abraham a great inheritance and heritage if he accepted this task but he would have to trust God for the eventual outcome. God was calling Abraham to the unknown; to give up all he had acquired and journey to a land he had never seen. Abraham obeyed, by faith.

Years ago I knew that God was calling me to ministry. I didn't know what to expect and to be honest I was scared. I assumed this meant God wanted to me to go somewhere as a missionary and, as selfish as this might sound, I did not want to give up hunting and fishing! Little did I know that a ministry involving my love for the outdoors is exactly what God was preparing for me down life's road. I couldn't see it but eventually this is where I ended up. True, God does call some folks to be missionaries and church pastors but I believe more often than not, God calls people to do things using the unique abilities, talents, gifts and passions he creates within them, you included. Years ago I would have never believed I get to do what I do today. I would never be doing what I do today if I hadn't obeyed God.

In a recent discussion about faith, risk, and adventure in my Adventure Leadership and Outdoor Ministry class at Liberty University, one of my students described faith this way: a Fantastic Adventure In Trusting Him, FAITH." It seems simple enough but it is incredibly profound. This truly is what God is calling each and every one of us to. He wants us to step up and step out on the incredible adventure of faith he is calling us to. What that journey or adventure looks like for each of us, I do not know because I do not know where it is God is calling you to go with your life. I do know this, however, just as in the life of Abraham, God promises indescribable reward and fulfillment for those who obey and by faith step out. The road may look long and leading to nowhere, the outcome uncertain, but that is just part of the adventure. When you finally arrive at the place God is calling you to go you can then look back from where you have come and it will make the experience all that much greater.

So how big is your faith? Big enough to trust God to do what he wants you to do and go where he wants you to go? There is no more perfect place to be than in the middle of God's will for your life. Lace up your boots, grab your pack, and let's journey there together.

In God's wildness lies the hope of the world - the great fresh unblighted, unredeemed wilderness. The galling harness of civilization drops off, and wounds heal ere we are aware. — John Muir

Endurance for the Backcountry

. *...because you know that the testing of your faith produces perseverance.* James 1:3 NIV

per ·se ·ver ·ance

1. steady persistence in a course of action, a purpose, a state, etc., especially in spite of difficulties, obstacles, or discouragement.

2. Theology: continuance in a state of grace to the end, leading to eternal salvation.

No one really likes to be tested. In school at least, students get the opportunity to study for the tests they take, giving them the chance to hopefully perform well. In life it seems, tests often are presented to us with little or no warning and we are faced with situations where we either have to find the stamina to make it through or we give up and fail. Although we might understand testing "produces perseverance," it is often of very little consolation at the moment we are facing the crisis situation.

Once the crisis or test has passed, however, we can look back at the situation and see how we are better because of it. Even if you did not perform well you still managed to learn something about yourself and life in general you will no doubt take with you into the next crisis or test you face. We have all been there. Every single person reading this today has at one time or another has had their life, their faith, tested and the very fact you are reading this means you came through it. You maybe bruised, bloodied, blistered, and battered, but you made it through.

I love the saying, "That which does not kill us only makes us stronger." Though I am not a big proponent of Friedrich

Nietzsche, the originator of this statement, there is still much truth to it. We don't gain physical endurance by sitting still. We have to exercise. Furthermore, people don't begin an exercise routine by running a marathon. You work up to it. In the same way, good hunters, especially those of us from the east, know if they truly want to be successful on a western mountain elk or sheep hunt they are going to have to put in some work ahead of time to build the endurance necessary to climb the mountains, with a pack, and get to where the big animals live.

The better shape you are in the further into the backcountry you can successfully go. The further back you go the better chance you have of seeing more and bigger game because you have left much of your much less well-prepared and conditioned competition behind. Likewise, our faith is no good unless it is exercised and conditioned. The sooner you realize that, the better off you are and the greater chance you have coming out the other side of whatever situation life throws at you successfully.

When your faith is tested, when life deals you a hard blow, recognize it for what it is, a test. Don't quit, don't give up. Jerry Falwell was famous for this saying, *"You do not measure a man's greatness by his talent or wealth, as the world does, but rather by what it takes to discourage him. It is always too early to quit."* You must press on and push through and afterwards you will realize just how much stronger you are because of it.

Sure it might be painful and it might leave scars but scars remain simply to remind us what we have come through and can serve to encourage us the next time we face another painful or endurance building experience. Just as in exercise, we first break down the muscle in order to rebuild it and make it stronger.

Remember, what doesn't kill you, makes you stronger. It is true in exercise, in life, and in faith. If you don't quit, testing will produce endurance that will see you through the hard times and endurance that will get you where you want to go; even to the backcountry. Maybe I will see you there!

Do not go where the path may lead. Go instead where there is no path and leave a trail.

— Ralph Waldo Emerson

Has Your Camp Become too Comfortable?

The LORD our God said to us in Horeb, 'You have stayed long enough at this mountain.' Deuteronomy 1:6 ESV

One of the hardest things about backpacking is moving on after you have found a perfect campsite; one that is flat, out of the wind, close to water and close to sustenance. Locations like that are hard to leave. They are comfortable, secure, and provide a sense of peace. The problem is eventually you have to strike camp and move on. If you don't, you will never reach your destination, you will eventually run out of supplies, and your perfect campsite will soon become a liability.

It's easy to get comfortable. We get involved in our routines such as work, school, church on Sundays, and going to the gym three days a week and we are content. Our routines are familiar and become as comfortable as an old sweatshirt. There is nothing wrong with comfortable until comfortable becomes complacency. Worse still is when comfortable becomes just a more polite term for stagnant.

It is vitally important to recognize when we have stayed long enough at a particular point in life. We were not created to be sedentary. We are part of grand adventure called life and to fully experience what it is God has in store for us we must be willing to move outside of our comfort zones. When we stay in one place for too long, our faith gets weak and our spiritual muscles atrophy. We slowly begin to waste away and rot in place. But while we rot, we are at least comfortable, right?

Just as God spoke to his people at Horeb and told them they had been comfortable long enough and to get moving, we too must recognize when our routine and contentment actually distract us from doing that which God would have us to do. We are too comfortable to move. Some of you know in your hearts right now God is telling you it is time to move; whether it is a physical move to a new location or a new job, or spiritually because you have been stuck in a rut. Instead you choose to stay where you are because it is "easier".

No doubt God's people faced uncertainly and challenge when they left the comfortable mountain even though God promised he would take care of them. After all it is the uncertainly and risk we face when we move away from the comfortable that truly makes our walk of faith the adventure it is. It is having to depend fully on God that reveals to us just how big and powerful he really is. You are not alone in this. I, too, get comfortable and have to remind myself of this as well.

Maybe you truly are right where God wants you right now in terms of location or vocation. If that is the case, great! But still I challenge you to look for those areas in your life where you have become too comfortable. Maybe it's time to volunteer in a new ministry at your church. Maybe it's time to start a new devotion or quiet time plan in God's Word instead of the same one you have been doing for years. Maybe it is time to meet a new group of friends or join a new small group at church. I don't know what it is with which you have become too comfortable but I am sure there is a routine in your life keeping you from fully experiencing all that God wants for you simply because it is easier.

What is God asking you to do? Is it time to move out of your comfort zone? Is your comfortable life keeping you from experiencing all that God wants you to experience? Maybe it is time to strike camp, tighten your laces, grab your pack, and move on down the trail. I bet God has something amazing waiting for you down the trail.

See you in the backcountry.

Solitude begins with a time and a place for God, and God alone. If we really believe not only that God exists but also that God is actively present in our lives-- healing, teaching and guiding-- we need to set aside a time and space to give God our undivided attention. (Matt 6:6) — Henri J.M. Nouwen

Take a Walk on the Wild Side

Immediately the Spirit drove Him into the wilderness. Mark 1:12 NKJV

There is just something about the wilderness that creates an incredibly rich environment for personal growth, change, and deep introspection. Getting away from the distractions of daily life such as phones, email, TV and even other people provides us an opportunity to truly focus on what is going on around us and in us. The wilderness can also be a place where we face our greatest tests in life; physically, mentally, and spiritually. It is in the wilderness where we see just how small we are (and our problems) and just how big God truly is.

It is interesting, and I believe significant, that the wilderness is where the earthly ministry of Jesus was launched. The preparation he underwent...prefaced in Mark 1:12. This experience set the stage for the three-year ministry Jesus led here on earth.

As we trace the recorded life of Jesus we find that over 90% of his ministry took place outdoors. I don't believe it is mere coincidence this is the case. I believe Jesus knew something about the benefits of being outdoors and leading lives outside.

I challenge you to study the life of Christ to see for yourself just how many times he invoked the natural surroundings as he taught by way of illustration. Study the geography as well to better understand the environment or surroundings in which he taught. Sometimes I wonder if he did not intentionally frame many of the experiences we read about in scripture within outdoor settings, in such a way it was impossible for those surrounding him not to see the Creator's hand in it.

It is also well documented in scripture that when Jesus wanted to be alone, needed to pray or to refresh his spirit the wilderness is where he would retreat. Many of us are the same way. Sometimes we just feel the need to get away and when we do it is often to a particular place outdoors, a stream, a giant rock, or a bench in a park we go to think and pray.

Wilderness means different things to different people. There is a legal definition of wilderness which holds special significance to public land managers, use planners, and others involved in the conservation of and recreation on public lands. However, for many people, wilderness means something entirely different.

Wilderness is simply wildness and although it could be a vast track of western land far removed from human influence it is more than likely somewhere close to where you are. Wilderness can be very subjective depending on the individual. It could be a small woodlot or a local park close to home just as easy as it as it could be a remote area in the Rio Grande National Forest or the Grand Tetons.

Regardless of where it is for you, the benefits of wilderness, or wild places, are nothing short of amazing. Being able to get away to a spot, whether near or far, surrounded by God's handiwork, free from distraction, and human interference puts you in a place where you can truly focus on God and hear what he is saying. Your senses become much more alive and focused and suddenly it makes sense; you are never closer to God himself than when you are in the very midst of that which his very hand created.

The wilderness, whatever this term may mean to you, is a truly remarkable place and your ability to tune into what God is saying to you can be accomplished there like no other place. The Bible is full of examples of how God spoke to his people and changed their lives through wilderness experience. Maybe it is time for you to get away. Maybe you have been longing to hear what God is trying to tell you but the distractions of daily life, technology, etc. are keeping you from receiving a clear message. Maybe it is time for you to turn your phone off, grab a pack and take a walk on the wild side with God. No doubt, you'll be glad you did.

Nature is full of genius, full of the divinity; so that not a snowflake escapes its fashioning hand.

— Henry David Thoreau

Why Worship?

"Worthy are you, our Lord and God, to receive glory and honor and power, for you created all things, and by your will they existed and were created." Revelation 4:11 ESV

Why do we worship? Why should we worship? What is worship?

Worship is an outward expression of an inward realization of who God is and all he has done. When we truly face the reality that all things are created by God and nothing exists outside of his perfect will we then, then and only then, can understand just how fortunate we are. It is this reality which adds meaning and depth to our worship response. Maybe it would help to add emphasis to Revelation 4:11:

Our Lord and God, You are WORTHY to receive glory and honor and power, BECAUSE You have CREATED ALL things, AND BECAUSE of YOUR WILL they exist and were created.

This makes understanding a bit clearer.

When we look around we see God's handiwork. Who among us hasn't been amazed at the natural beauty he has created? A beautiful sunrise, an amber sunset, snow-capped mountain peaks, a stream, a green meadow, a turkey's gobble and valley's expanse are all testament to the fact God created them and that he wanted to create them. The Bible tells us God created all these things for his pleasure, for his glory, and called them all, "very good". Furthermore, he could have created colorless, black and white world had he wanted. Instead, he created a world rich in color and in high definition because the world he created is a reflection of who he is.

When we look in the mirror we also see God's handiwork and we are further reminded how each of us is created to worship. We are part of the very same world that he created and willed into being. You are here because God wanted you to be here. By his will, you exist. By his hands you are made.

In addition, have you noticed that humans are the only members of God's creation with the capacity to outwardly express their worship? I am sure is no accident. It would seem then, we have a responsibility to do what it is God gave us the capacity to do in response to who he is and what he has done.

The concept of "worship" today can often become a confusing mixture of emotion, performance, and vain posturing. The where and when of worship is often the central theme, revolving around a building and a style of music. Forgotten are the why, the what, and most importantly, the Who.

When you need to be reminded, just look around. We worship because he is worthy.

Always do what you are afraid to do.

— Ralph Waldo Emerson

What's the Risk?

...If I perish, I perish. Esther 4:16 NIV

Have you ever taken a risk? I am not talking about a risk that didn't mean much in the way of consequence; I mean a risk in which failure could cost you dearly, maybe even your life? Maybe it was a risk you chose and had time to plan for, such as climbing a mountain, an extended backcountry trip, or kayaking swift and dangerous water. For others, maybe the risk was not one you chose but instead chose you. You didn't have time to think or plan, you just had to respond on instinct and training such as a soldier in battle, or a police officer or firefighter running into danger to save public lives. What would it take for you to make a conscious decision on a risk that at best offered a 50/50 chance you would survive? What predicating factors would cause you to take such an extreme risk where you would say, "If I perish, I perish"?

Although we don't have space to delve deeply into the story of Queen Esther, she was forced into a position where she had to take a risk. Her people were at risk of a massive genocide on account of an evil, pride-filled, and deceptive advisor to her husband the king. In order for her to put her plan into motion, in an effort to save her people, Esther needed to make an unannounced and uninvited visit to the king. The issue at stake was the fact that in that day and in that culture a person, not even the queen, did such a thing. It often meant a swift death sentence for whoever chose to interrupt the king. Esther knew this all too well yet she also knew the risk of doing nothing was the certain slaughter of the Jews. She determined to visit the king while saying, "If I perish, I perish." Fortunately for Esther and her people, this story has a happy ending.

There are many truths about risk, but two in particular. First it forces us to use our faith. Secondly, are lives are richer because of it. Imagine how dull our lives would be if they were spent in fear, living in a cocoon seeking to avoid all risk and adventure.

God has been calling his people to take risks from the beginning. One need not look hard in either the Old or New Testaments to find numerous examples of people who took risks because God called them to. In almost every situation the potential consequence was life or death, not merely the possibility of a bad day. Each one understood the potential benefit outweighed the negative and the consequence of doing nothing far outweighed any negative still. In each situation, however, God was with them then every step of the way. God saw them through and their lives, as well as the lives of others, were richer for the experience.

What risk is God calling you to take? What giant step of faith has he placed in your path and are you willing to trust Him to see you through? Have you asked yourself the question, "What is the consequence if I don't take the risk?" The stakes may be high and the future uncertain, but this we know, God doesn't call us to failure. Remember, it is HIS will that is at stake here, not yours.

If God puts you to it, God will see you through it. And that is a no risk guarantee.

Everybody needs beauty as well as bread, places to play in and pray in, where nature may heal and give strength to body and soul alike. — John Muir

Under the Old Oak Tree

The angel of the Lord came and sat down under the oak ...
Judges 6:11 NIV

At first read I can understand you thinking this verse is not very inspirational or motivational. However, let's look at the verse in the context of what is going on; if you have a Bible, read the preceding verses and those that follow. The Israelites had been held captive by the Midianites for several years as punishment for their disobedience to God. The people had just recently repented and God promised them deliverance from their slave state. Despite the good news of God's promise, we see Gideon feverishly working away threshing wheat, out of sight of the Midianites, for fear they might steal it. One did not normally thresh wheat in a wine vat but that is exactly what Gideon was doing out of fear and no doubt he was working much harder than he would be had he been threshing wheat in the open. When the Angel of the Lord appeared, who most biblical scholars agree was a pre-incarnate Jesus Christ, God the Son, he didn't help Gideon with the threshing. Instead, he sat down in the shade, under a large, old, and well-known oak tree. While Gideon worked, God watched. While God was at rest, Gideon was stressed.

Eventually, the scripture tells us the Angel of the Lord got Gideon's attention and invited him to come and sit under the oak tree with him and share a meal. It wasn't until Gideon stopped his futile work, took a break, and sat alone with God under the old oak tree that he recognized exactly who we was resting with and the true ramification of what was really going on took hold. When Gideon stopped to commune with God, Gideon received his call from God.

37

How many of us are like Gideon? We know the promises God makes us, like God telling his people they'd be free, but we never really take time to internalize them and truly believe God at his word. Instead of focusing on God's promises we instead get preoccupied with attempting to solve life's problems. We go right on working, often in vain, instead of acknowledging the fact God is in control. We keep trying to fix our own problems and find our own answers despite the fact God has already said he has it covered. How many of us are hidden away in a figurative wine vat attempting to work out answers or solutions to life's biggest problems on our own, stressed out, worried, and unsure?

Maybe, what you need to do is stop. Stop what you are doing, stop trying to figure things out, and go sit under an old oak tree. Stop and listen intently and purposefully to the voice of God. Don't just hear what he says, listen. God has the answers and he knows just what you need. He knows exactly the purpose for which you have been created and he can't wait for you to fulfill that purpose. But as long as you keep busy, preoccupied with your own devices, you will never hear or see what God is trying to say or show you.

Slow down. Stop. Take a break. Pack a lunch and go sit and fellowship with God under that old oak tree. It's where Gideon met God and received his calling. It may just be where you do too.

God's love is manifest in the landscape as in a face.

— John Muir

Don't Miss the Forest on Account of the Trees

Jesus said to her, "I who speak to you am He." John 4:26 NKJV

Have you ever thought you lost your sunglasses only to realize you were wearing them? Have you ever been tracking an animal so intently that you missed the fact it was mere feet in front of you? Perhaps you missed a well-marked detour on a hike because "there was no way the marker was right." Maybe you have heard this expression, don't miss the forest on account of the trees? So often the signs are right there in front of us and we still miss them.

John 4 is one of if not my favorite chapters in the Bible. I love the account of Jesus meeting the Samaritan woman at the well. It is an amazing story of grace, hope, restoration and how God can transform and use anyone in spite of their past and self-apparent lack of self-esteem or self-worth. As the story goes, Jesus just so happens to be hanging out at a water-well, where he meets a Samaritan woman who had come to draw water in the heat of the day. The woman comes to draw water well after all the other women of the town do most likely on account of her sordid past; many women in the town probably didn't appreciate her and her reputation with the men. To begin the conversation, Jesus asks her for a drink. This was out of the ordinary as men did not normally associate like this with women in those times and especially Jews did not socialize with Samaritans. And for a rabbi to ask her, a woman with a stained life and well deserved repute, for a drink, something was definitely out of the ordinary. Thus began a conversation in which Jesus explained the scriptures, answered her questions, explained how he could give her "living water" with which she would never thirst again, and even told this woman all about her life and her current sinful situation. This was certainly no ordinary Jewish rabbi. There was something different about this man. Still she did not get it. Finally, the woman says she believes the Messiah, the one called Christ, will one day come and explain everything. It is then, in response, Jesus says, "I am He, the One speaking to you."

Then the light went on. It suddenly all made sense! The very one she had been waiting for was in fact standing in front of her all along. The Messiah she heard about just asked her for a drink of water. Fortunately, this story has an amazing and happy ending.

How often have you missed the signs from God even though they were right in front of you? So often we get fixated on the idea that in order for God to reveal himself, or his plan for our lives, it has to come as a big sign or other overwhelmingly obvious way. We go through our days looking for flashing billboards rather than those more likely indicators right at our feet; things we often step over or around in the search for the bigger, more attractive and more obvious signs. We ask God to use us to "make a difference in lives of his people" but ignore the single mother, the homeless, the homesick, the broken hearted, the traumatized veteran, or the fatherless kid down the street we see every day.

Sometimes we become so consumed with our past or our perceived lack of ability or education that we don't believe God can ever use us and instead we ignore the signs all around us. God gave you your story, no matter how sordid it may be and he can use for his glory. God put you where you are, right where you are, to make a difference in the lives of those around you. You don't have to have a church to pastor or a seminary degree to see God can use you anywhere. Ask yourself, "What is my story and how can God use it?" Ask yourself, "Where did God put me and how can he use me where I am at?" Then look around. Without a doubt, the answer has been there all along.

More importantly, for someone reading this, you may have heard about the Messiah, the Christ, and you may be searching for and waiting for that encounter to meet him so that you too can experience the same grace, hope, restoration, and transformation the woman at the well experienced. This is your time. You need no other sign.

Whatever you do, don't miss out on God's plan for you on account of your past. Don't bypass his purpose for your life while looking for billboards. Don't miss out on the Messiah on account of your search for meaning. In other words, don't miss the forest on account of the trees.

The signs are obvious.

To live a spiritual life we must first find the courage to enter into the desert of our loneliness and to change it by gentle and persistent efforts into a garden of solitude. The movement from loneliness to solitude, however, is the beginning of any spiritual life because it is the movement from the restless senses to the restful spirit, from the outward-reaching cravings to the inward-reaching search, from the fearful clinging to the fearless play."
— Henri J.M. Nouwen

Photo by Ken Lamb   www.northernshutter.com

It's About What Lies at the End of the Trail

For this light momentary affliction is preparing for us an eternal weight of glory beyond all comparison, 2 Corinthians 4:17 ESV

Blisters, mosquito bites, raw shoulders, hunger, and thirst. All of these things can plague us and cause discomfort on the trail. We can try and prepare for them but inevitably some form of irritation is going to work its way in and bug us the rest of our trip. As uncomfortable as these irritations might be, we still push on. Often times we don't have the option of quitting; there is nowhere else to go but ahead. It is these afflictions, however, that make completing our trek all that much more rewarding. We appreciate our success all that much more and that big juicy hamburger tastes so much better than we ever imagined after a week of eating granola and freeze-dried meals. It is an amazing sensation to complete our journey despite our affliction; almost euphoric.

The Apostle Paul was someone who knew something about affliction. He tells us in his writings how he had a figurative "thorn in the flesh," which nagged him most of his life (2 Corinthians 12:7-10). It didn't stop him but it certainly made his job that much harder. And then there were the bigger afflictions that came his way; shipwrecks, being left adrift at sea, prison, and beatings. Still, Paul was not deterred and remained on the steady course God had called him too. Paul said in Philippians 3:14, "I pursue as my goal the prize promised by God's heavenly call in Christ Jesus." Paul knew the prize was promised at the finish line, not the starting line, or anywhere in between. To claim it, he had to finish.

The path isn't promised to be an easy one or else we wouldn't appreciate it. Satan is going to do all he can to discourage you from finishing well by whatever means necessary. I love the promise in today's verse however; an <u>absolutely incomparable</u> weight of glory is in store for us when we finish. It is absolutely incomparable! How can you beat, absolutely incomparable? You can't. It is absolutely incomparable! It's better than the juicy burger after two weeks in the backcountry and it is more glorious than climbing to the top of Mt. Katahdin at the end of your 2000+ mile trek on the Appalachian Trail.

We are always better off preparing ourselves, physically and spiritually, to mitigate affliction on our journey but we can never totally eliminate it. What do we do when we are afflicted? We keep going. You lance the blister, wrap duct tape around it, and keep going. We rest when we need to, get help along the way but we don't stop. We can't turn back, and we can't quit. To quit is to give up and to give up is to say God's not big enough to see you through.

We must keep focused on our goal of finishing well the journey we are on. We will fight through our affliction and blisters knowing our current discomforts are making finishing our journey all that much sweeter. Remember, the absolutely incomparable glory that awaits us at the end. God never promised us the journey we are on would be easy, only that it would be worth it.

Finish well my friends. Finish well.

We are always getting ready to live but never living.

— **Ralph Waldo Emerson**

Awesome God

...and to know this love that surpasses knowledge – that you may be filled to the measure of all the fullness of God. Ephesians 3:19 NIV

Do you remember as a kid wanting something so bad that you told your parents that if you could somehow get this one thing you wouldn't ask for anything for your birthday or Christmas? In your mind you knew that if you could get whatever it is you had your mind on you would somehow be completed. Did you ever get it? Were you truly completed? Did you still have a wish list of things that maybe you "forgot about" when your birthday or Christmas rolled around?

What about outdoors? How many of us have ever hiked the entire Appalachian Trail, caught a nine-pound bass, shot a big buck, or successfully paddled a seemingly impossible stretch of water and then said to ourselves, "I am now complete," and then hung up our gear content to never step foot on the trail, water, or in the woods again? Of course not! We simply move on to the next bigger challenge. The truth is, as great as they might seem, none of these accomplishments fulfill us completely. Where these things might fill one hole, they just open another needing to be filled.

Ephesians 3:19 tells us of one of the most amazing qualities of God you and I can share in, his love. So incredible is his love that the verse tells us it surpasses knowledge; meaning it exceeds human comprehension. His love for us is so immense we cannot possibly even begin to understand it. Not only that, but the same incomprehensible love is waiting to fill you completely. The verse literally means to be "crammed completely full". What do you think the implications would be if the world would ever fully understand it is the love of God, and his love alone which can complete us? Greed and selfishness would end. There would be no substance abuse. Relationships would last and divorce would be a thing of the past. There would be no room left in our lives for anything else to "complete" us because every void would be fully satisfied by the love of Christ.

As impossible as it seems, the reality is it is possible. It starts with you and me realizing just how amazing God's love toward us truly is and by opening our hearts, allowing them to be crammed full of this love until we are completely filled with it. As we allow more and more of God's love to fill us, it will eventually push anything else out that might be holding us back from experiencing the full extent of his love. Remember, it was God's love for us that allowed Jesus to be crucified, to die for us as a ransom for our sin. It was his love for us that held Jesus on the cross until this work could be completed. It is this same amazing, powerful, unconditional, love that can fill your life to its absolute fullest.

Pursue your dreams, your passions, and your goals. Remember, all the success and all the accomplishments in the world can never entirely complete or fulfill you personally. Only the love of God can do that. Knowing you are already fully loved, fully complete, and totally fulfilled before you ever attempt to fulfill your dreams and goals will ultimately make all those accomplishments just that much sweeter and certainly more meaningful.

"The spiritual life does not remove us from the world but leads us deeper into it"
— Henri J.M. Nouwen

What Does the Condition of Your Gear Say About You?

Enoch walked faithfully with God; then he was no more, because God took him away. Genesis 5:24 NIV

Outdoor people are pretty easy to spot. They often stand out in a crown on account of their technical pants, hiking boots, carabineers dangling from belt loops, backpack daisy chains, Leatherman tools on their sides, nalgene or aluminum water bottles, and labels such as Patagonia, North Face, Merrell, Kenetrek, Kifaru, Brunton, Primus, and Kryptek decorating their gear and wardrobes. Yet a true outdoor person can tell who is a "real" outdoors person by the condition of their gear. Is it new or well-used? Does the person wearing it look like they just stepped out of an REI ad? Anyone can wear the gear; it takes someone special to actually put it to use. And no one appreciates a poser.

Enoch didn't just talk about it, he really did it. The words in the original language say that Enoch walked continuously alongside God. It was part of a routine. I am not sure what it was that set Enoch apart from every other person on earth at the time and caused God to single him out, but there must have been something pretty special and it certainly was more than just Enoch keeping up with appearances. God didn't go on daily walks with just anyone and he would have seen right through the charade had there been one. I wonder if other people knew about Enoch's daily walks with God. I wonder if people could pick him out in the crowd. I wonder if Enoch was known around town as "that guy". Not because of what he wore, but because of where he had been; with God.

How amazing it would be to be like Enoch and have that kind of a relationship with God. It's one thing for us to go out for a walk or hike through the woods and pray along our way but imagine having God literally right beside you! No doubt our time spent along with God can be amazingly personal and intimate times in which not only we speak to God but he speaks to us. What can we do, however, to make those times even more intimate? What stands in the way of our having such an intense, intimate relationship with God, like that with Enoch, he would want to walk literally alongside us. More importantly, after we spend time with God can others notice? It is obvious to others where we've been or are we just wearing the impressive labels?

I love how the story of Enoch ends, *"he was not there because God took him."* One day Enoch was there walking along with God and then he wasn't. Nothing is recorded about Enoch's death and the number of years he lived because one day he was just gone. God took him. There is no doubt God enjoyed Enoch's company and their daily walks. I have to wonder if at the end of one of those long days of walking, as the sun began to set and it was time for Enoch to go home, if God just didn't turn to Enoch and say, "You know, it's getting late, and we have walked a long way together. We are closer to my home than yours. Why not just come home with me?"

We should all long for a special relationship with God that makes us unique, like Enoch. Our time spent with God should be evident to others. We should all strive to be so close, and to walk so far with God that at the end of the day, we are closer to his house than ours.

How close we are to getting there will no doubt be evident, not in fancy labels, but in the condition of our well-worn gear.

Trail Talk: Eliminating Distractions

If Moses had been using his smart phone to text friends, send emails, update his Facebook status, or post to his Twitter timeline would he have ever seen the burning the bush? Like most of us, Moses probably would have been so intent on studying the device in his hand he would have walked right on by the message God was trying to give him. Exodus 3:1-12 tells the story. Take note of how in verses 2 & 3 Moses noticed the bush and made the decision to go see what it was all about. In verse 4, when God saw that Moses was being attentive, he revealed Himself by speaking to him.

How many of us miss the signs God places in our lives because of the distractions we refuse to distance ourselves from? If we are honest, it is more of refusal on our part. We make a decision to let many of the things of this world become priorities on which we fixate to the neglect of everything else. This is obviously one of the benefits of removing ourselves from civilization and into the backcountry; there are no electrical outlets and few, if any, opportunities for us to remain "plugged in" and distracted. Of course it is not just technology; there are many other seemingly harmless things, which if we allow them, can overtake our lives and priorities as well.

Answer the following questions.

Be honest. What are some ways you find yourself distracted and inattentive to God? What are the things in your life that are making it impossible for you to see the plans God has for you?

What are other examples in the Bible where people have eliminated distractions and taken time to get alone with God in the wilderness or other wild and natural places in order to hear or better understand what God is calling them to?

How is your life like theirs?

What can you do to eliminate or at least minimize distractions so you can be more attentive to God's voice?

What is the one thing you believe God might be urging you to do but have been too distracted to listen?

Pray

God, please help me to see the distractions in my life that are keeping me from spending time with you and listening to what you are trying to say to me. Help me to minimize or eliminate those distractions so I can be more attentive to you and your will for my life. Allow this time, alone with you in your creation, to be the start of a renewed relationship with you. Amen.

Trail Talk: Getting Close

Do you feel better connected to God when you are outdoors? What is it about being outside that seems to draw you closer to God? There are numerous instances in scripture where God spoke to his people or revealed aspects of Himself to his people in an outdoor environment. One of the first, and one of my favorite "Aha!" moments occurs early in the Bible and involves Abraham.

God had decided Abraham was going to be the father of the great nation of Israel. Abraham didn't know this yet and God had to tell him. The account is found in Genesis chapter 15.

Abraham is in his tent when God speaks to him and tells him the news. Abraham is full of doubt as he has no children and no one to carry on as an heir except for a slave. Instead of trying to reason with Abraham, what does God do? Verse five tells us, "He took him outside…"

God took Abraham outside and told him to look up at the stars and try and count them. He promised Abraham, despite his current childless circumstance, his offspring would be just as numerous. God used his creation as an object to get his point across.

To do so, he had to move Abraham outside. Abraham could not see just how big and vast God was as long as he remained in his tent. When he saw just how big and marvelous God was, he believed and thus began one of the first major outdoor adventures in scripture.

Answer these questions.

What is it about being outdoors that draws you closer to God?

How does God use the outdoors to reveal parts of Himself to you?

What aspects of God's creation do you see that are reminders of just how big God is?

What aspects of the God's creation are reminders of God's amazing promises to you?

Pray

God, thank you for your amazing creation, the opportunity to be in it, a part of it, and enjoy it to its fullest extent. Help me not to take it for granted. Please open my eyes and my heart to see just how big and marvelous you are as well as the plans and promises you have for me as you reveal yourself to me through all that which your hands have created. Amen.

Trail Talk: Savor The Flavor

Taste and see that the Lord is good. Psalm 34:8 HCSB

I apologize in advance if this makes you hungry, especially if you are on the trail and down to last few handfuls of trail-mix. However, one of my favorite things about heading into backcountry is preparing in advance my daily menu. Gathering tortillas, hard sausage, cheese, peanut butter, and an assortment of freeze dried foods, MRE's, and of course coffee, is fun. But the best part of preparing your food is when you get to enjoy it. A good meal at the end of the day or some calories part way through can be a truly amazing, refreshing, and enjoyable experience. When the opportunity arises and I am able to add fresh fish or meat to the menu it is a bonus. Two things are for sure; food tastes better when you are hungry and when you take time to actually enjoy it.

I love the words of the Psalmist, "Taste and see that the Lord is good." How often do you take time to really savor the Lord? It is easy for most of us when we are hungry to reach for whatever foods are close in order to feed our cravings. How often, though, do we honestly stop to taste it and savor its complexities? I think our relationship with God is very much the same way. We run to Him when we have a craving or we need a quick fix and then put Him away once we feel satisfied. We really never take the time to consider his complexities and just how eternally satisfying he is.

Ask yourself the following questions and be honest in your response.

How often do you crave God?

Do you run to merely get your "fix" of God or is he instead a source of constant nourishment and satisfaction? What can you do differently?

As funny as this might sound, how might you describe how the Lord tastes? How does he satisfy you?

"I am the bread of life," Jesus told them. "No one who comes to Me will ever be hungry, and no one who believes in Me will ever be thirsty again." John 6:35

Trail Talk: Essential Survival Gear

Of the items I stress to my students they make sure they carry into woods, the one I tell them they must not skimp on quality is a good knife. Preferably, they carry more than one. In my opinion, it is the most essential of all survival tools. With nothing more than a good knife a person in an emergency situation can build a shelter, start a fire, get food, and if the unfortunate need arises, can even protect themselves. There is not much a good knife can't do in the hands of resourceful person. A poor quality knife, however, is not much good. Sure, it might work for a while, but in a true emergency situation, under stress, it will likely fail. If it doesn't break it may quickly lose its edge and ultimately its effectiveness. Much like a poor quality knife, we often compromise in our spiritual growth and care to the point that we lose our effectiveness and often fail and fall when the chips are down and we are placed under the stress of life.

Many neglect time spent in God's word. Instead, the daily devotions you find in your email inbox, a podcast or two, and maybe the latest bestselling book become substitutes. We neglect time for ourselves in the pages of God's Word while instead allowing someone else to handle the task for us. It is an easier way out for many and the cost is cheap as it requires little time and sacrifice on one's behalf. For many, the pages of a Bible are never opened between Sundays. The fact is, all the extra stuff, the books, podcasts, etc. are great, but there is no substitute for spending time alone in God's Word. It is one of the primary means in which God communicates to us. Studying and memorizing scripture are essential to our personal spiritual survival.

Hebrews 4:12 tells says," For the word of God *is* living and powerful, and sharper than any two-edged sword, piercing even to the division of soul and spirit, and of joints and marrow, and is a discerner of the thoughts and intents of the heart" (NKJV). God's Word is essential to your spiritual development. It cuts to the core, is eternally relevant, and tells us more about ourselves than we may know, or want to know. It is our greatest tool for spiritual survival and growth. Don't neglect it.

Ask yourself these questions and answer honestly.

How much value do you put into God's word?

Do you seek out meaningful time in God's Word for personal study or reflection?

What has God's Word taught you about yourself?

What are some steps you might take to improve the quality and quantity of time you spend reading and studying God's Word?

The Waterproof Bible

Another item I have trained myself to never enter the woods without is a Bible. I have placed copies of the Waterproof Bible (www.BardinMarsee.com) in each of my packs so no matter where I go and which pack I grab I always have a copy securely packed away. Available in a number of translations, the Waterproof Bible is virtually indestructible and it floats! You just never know when and where God might speak and I figure if I am ever lost in the wilderness, a Bible is the one book I would want with me. After all, a significant portion is about people wandering in the wilderness!

Selected Verses from the Bible
Relevant to the Outdoors and Spiritual Formation

Adapted in part from Dr. Ashley Denton; Christian Outdoor Leadership

http://www.outdoorleaders.com/outdoor-ministry-resources/

Edited and added-to by Doug Gilmer

Genesis 1 & 2 - The creation account

Genesis 2:15 - God's command for man to watch over and care for his creation

Genesis 12:1-20 - Abraham called to mission of faith

Genesis 15:1-21 - The Lord takes Abraham outside as an object lesson and to affirm his promise

Genesis 22:1-19 - God tests Abraham by commanding him to sacrifice Isaac

Genesis 32:22-32 - Jacob Wrestles with God

Exodus 2:15-25 - Moses escapes to Midian

Exodus 3:1-9 - Moses and the Burning Bush

Exodus 3:1 - 4:20 - The mission of Moses

Exodus 15:22-27 - The Lord provides water

Exodus 16:1-7 - The Lord provides manna

Exodus 16:8-21 - The Lord provides meat

Exodus 18:17-27 - Jethro counsels Moses on the importance of teamwork

Exodus 19:1-25 - Moses meets God on Mount Sinai

Exodus 20 - The Ten Commandments

Exodus 24:15-18 - Moses and the Glory of the LORD on Mount Sinai

Exodus 34:29-35 - Moses' face shines after being in the presence of God on the mountain

Numbers 13:1-33 - The twelve spies sent to explore the new land.

Numbers 20:8-14 – The motives of Moses are tested, and he fails

Deuteronomy 34:1-12 -The death and burial of Moses in the wilderness

Joshua 3 - Israel crosses Jordan under God's guidance

Joshua 4 - Joshua builds a memorial stones at the Jordan River to serve as a reminder of God's faithfulness in wilderness.

Judges 7:1-25 - God proves to Gideon his power and resourcefulness in a wilderness battle

I Samuel 17 - David and Goliath

I Samuel 23 & 24 - Saul pursues David into the wilderness.

I Kings 19 - Elijah flees from Jezebel into the wilderness

Job 38, 39 - God speaks of nature, its beings, his greatness and sovereignty.

Job 40:15-24 - God's power shown in creatures

Psalm 8 - The Lord's glory and majesty and man's dignity

Psalm 19 - Creation proclaims God's majesty.

Psalm 33 – Worshipping the God of creation

Psalm 104 – God's care and creativity in his creation

Psalm 139 - God's omnipresence and omniscience

Psalm 148 – Let all of creation praise the Lord

Isaiah 40 - The greatness of God

Isaiah 43:7 - We were created for God's glory.

Isaiah 49 - God's faithfulness and salvation extend to the ends of the earth

Isaiah 65:17-25 - The promise of a new heaven and the new earth

Jonah The story of how Jonah ran from God and how a whale intervened

Matthew 2:1-12 - The adoration of the infant Jesus by the three wise men

Luke 2:8-20 - The adoration of the infant Jesus by the shepherds from the fields

Matthew 3:1-6 - John the Baptist prepares the way for Jesus' ministry

Matthew 3:13-17 - The baptism of Jesus

Matthew 6:25-34 – God's care for his creation is evidence of his care for us

Luke 4:1-13 - The temptation of Jesus Christ in the wilderness

Luke 5:1-11 - The call of the first disciples and the miraculous catch of fish

John 4:4-42 - Encountering the woman at the well

Mark 1:35-38 - Jesus retreats alone to a quiet place to pray and then begins his journey.

Mark 3:13-19 - Jesus chooses the Twelve Disciples; the original small group.

Mark 4:35-41 - Stilling the storm

Matthew 8:18-22 - On the radical call to follow Jesus

Mark 6:30-31 - The return of the Apostles small group mentoring

Mark 6:45-52 – Jesus walks on the water and the test of Peter's faith

Mark 8:1-10 - Four thousand are fed

Luke 9:28-36 - The Transfiguration

John 6:1-15 - Five thousand are fed

John 10:40-42 Jesus withdraws across the Jordan River

Mark 14:32-42 - Jesus retreats in the Garden of Gethsemane

Luke 24:13-35 - Jesus appears to the two disciples on the road to Emmaus

John 21:1-14 - Jesus appears by the Sea of Galilee

Matthew 28:16-20 - The Great Commission

Luke 24:44-53 - Jesus' last words and ascension to heaven from the mountain

Acts 9:1-9 – Saul (Paul's) conversion on the road to Damascus

Acts 10: 9-15 – Peter's vision and God's instruction that nothing He created is unclean to eat

Acts 27:1-28:6 – Paul's sailing adventure

Romans 1:20-21 - God's revelation to all men through creation

I Corinthians 9:24-28 – Physical and spiritual discipline needed to compete

II Corinthians 4:16-18 – Do not lose heart

II Corinthians 12:7-10 – God's grace is sufficient in our weakness

Philippians 1:20-26 – Perspective; to live is Christ, to die is gain.

Philippians 3:14 – Keep your eyes on the goal

Philippians 4:13 – All things are possible through Him who gives strength

Hebrews 4:13 – God sees all things in his creation

Revelation 21:1-8 – A new heaven and a new earth

Revelation 22: 1-5 – The Garden of Eden restored

How Great Thou Art
Carl Boberg-1886

O Lord my God, When I in awesome wonder,
 Consider all the worlds Thy Hands have made;
 I see the stars, I hear the rolling thunder,
 Thy power throughout the universe displayed.

Then sings my soul, My Saviour God, to Thee,
 How great Thou art, How great Thou art.
 Then sings my soul, My Saviour God, to Thee,
 How great Thou art, How great Thou art!

When through the woods, and forest glades I wander,
 And hear the birds sing sweetly in the trees.
 When I look down, from lofty mountain grandeur
 And see the brook, and feel the gentle breeze.

Then sings my soul, My Saviour God, to Thee,
 How great Thou art, How great Thou art.
 Then sings my soul, My Saviour God, to Thee,
 How great Thou art, How great Thou art!

And when I think, that God, His Son not sparing;
 Sent Him to die, I scarce can take it in;
 That on the Cross, my burden gladly bearing,
 He bled and died to take away my sin.

Then sings my soul, My Saviour God, to Thee,
 How great Thou art, How great Thou art.
 Then sings my soul, My Saviour God, to Thee,
 How great Thou art, How great Thou art!

When Christ shall come, with shout of acclamation,
 And take me home, what joy shall fill my heart.
 Then I shall bow, in humble adoration,

And then proclaim: "My God, how great Thou art!"

Then sings my soul, My Saviour God, to Thee,
 How great Thou art, How great Thou art.
 Then sings my soul, My Saviour God, to Thee,
 How great Thou art, How great Thou art!

This is My Father's World
Maltbie Babcock-circa 1901

This is my Father's world, and to my listening ears
All nature sings, and round me rings the music of the spheres.
This is my Father's world: I rest me in the thought
Of rocks and trees, of skies and seas;
His hand the wonders wrought.

This is my Father's world, the birds their carols raise,
The morning light, the lily white, declare their Maker's praise.
This is my Father's world: He shines in all that's fair;
In the rustling grass I hear Him pass;
He speaks to me everywhere.

This is my Father's world. O let me ne'er forget
That though the wrong seems oft so strong, God is the ruler yet.
This is my Father's world: the battle is not done;
Jesus who died shall be satisfied,
And earth and heaven be one.

All Creatures of Our God and King

Text: Francis of Assisi, ca. 1225; trans. by William H. Draper, 1925, adapt. 1987

All creatures of our God and King,
lift up your voice and with us sing,
O praise ye! Alleluia!
O brother sun with golden beam,
O sister moon with silver gleam!
O praise ye! O praise ye!
Alleluia! Alleluia! Alleluia!

O brother wind, air, clouds, and rain,
by which all creatures ye sustain,
O praise ye! Alleluia!
Thou rising morn, in praise rejoice,
ye lights of evening, find a voice!
O praise ye! O praise ye!
Alleluia! Alleluia! Alleluia!

O sister water, flowing clear,
make music for thy Lord to hear,
Alleluia! Alleluia!
O brother fire who lights the night,
providing warmth, enhancing sight,
O praise ye! O praise ye!
Alleluia! Alleluia! Alleluia!

Dear mother earth, who day by day
unfoldest blessings on our way,
Alleluia! Alleluia!
The flowers and fruits that in thee grow,
let them God's glory also show!
O praise ye! O praise ye!
Alleluia! Alleluia! Alleluia!

All ye who are of tender heart,

forgiving others, take your part,
O praise ye! Alleluia!
Ye who long pain and sorrow bear,
praise God and on him cast your care!
O praise ye! O praise ye!
Alleluia! Alleluia! Alleluia!

And thou, our sister, gentle death,
waiting to hush our latest breath,
Alleluia! Alleluia!
Thou leadest home the child of God,
and Christ our Lord the way has trod,
O praise ye! O praise ye!
Alleluia! Alleluia! Alleluia!

Let all things their Creator bless,
and worship him in humbleness,
O praise ye! Alleluia!
Praise, praise the Father, praise the Son,
and praise the Spirit, Three in One!
O praise ye! O praise ye!
Alleluia! Alleluia! Alleluia!

Create Again

Aaron Shust and Dan Hannon

Separated from night
You spoke and then there was light
They point to You

Divided water from land
Bowing to Your command
They point to You

The sun that's blazing at noon
And every phase of the moon
They point to You.

A baby's cry and the way
A sunset closes the day
They point to You.

For You're the only One worth praising
More radiant than earth and sky
And everyday that I survey Your creation
I see why I see why

God of everything I see,
Come create again in me
You were yesterday
and You will always be
So take each breath that I breathe
And be the life that I bleed
Create again in me

The storm that's raging at sea

The little child on her knees
They point to You

Your grace that's poured out on me
The sacrifice on a tree
They point to You
Your Word vaults across the sky

From sunrise to sunset
Melting the ice, scorching the desert
Warm our hearts to faith
Create again in me

Indescribable

Jesse Reeves and Laura Story
©2004 worshiptogether.com songs
sixsteps Music
Gleaning Publishing

From the highest of heights to the depths of the sea
Creation's revealing Your majesty
From the colors of fall to the fragrance of spring
Every creature unique in the song that it sings
All exclaiming

Indescribable, uncontainable,
You placed the stars in the sky and You know them by name.
You are amazing God
All powerful, untamable,
Awestruck we fall to our knees as we humbly proclaim
You are amazing God

Who has told every lightning bolt where it should go
Or seen heavenly storehouses laden with snow
Who imagined the sun and gives source to its light
Yet conceals it to bring us the coolness of night
None can fathom

Indescribable, uncontainable,
You placed the stars in the sky and You know them by name
You are amazing God
All powerful, untamable,
Awestruck we fall to our knees as we humbly proclaim
You are amazing God

Indescribable, uncontainable,

You placed the stars in the sky and You know them by name.
You are amazing God
All powerful, untamable,
Awestruck we fall to our knees as we humbly proclaim
You are amazing God
Indescribable, uncontainable,
You placed the stars in the sky and You know them by name.
You are amazing God
Incomparable, unchangeable
You see the depths of my heart and You love me the same
You are amazing God
You are amazing God

God of Wonders

Marc Birdsong and Steve Hindalong
©2000 New Spring
Never Say Never Songs
Storm Boy Music
Meaux Mercy

Lord of all creation Of water, earth, and sky
The heavens are Your tabernacle
Glory to the Lord on High

God of wonders, beyond our galaxy
You are holy, holy
The universe declares Your majesty
You are holy, holy

Lord of heaven and earth

Early in the morning I will celebrate the light
And as I stumble through the darkness
I will call Your name by night

God of wonders, beyond our galaxy
You are holy, holy
The universe declares Your majesty
You are holy, holy

Lord of heaven and earth
Hallelujah to the Lord of heaven and earth

God of wonders, beyond our galaxy
You are holy, holy
Precious Lord, reveal Your heart to me
Father holy, holy
The universe declares Your majesty

You are holy, holy, holy, holy

Hallelujah to the Lord of heaven and earth (6X)

Lord of heaven and earth
Lord of heaven and earth

Early in the morning I will celebrate the light
and as I stumble through the darkness
I will call your name by night

God of wonders beyond our galaxy
You are holy, holy
The universe declares your majesty
You are holy, holy

Lord of heaven and earth
Lord of heaven and earth

Halleluiah to the Lord of heaven and earth
Halleluiah to the Lord of heaven and earth

God of wonders beyond our galaxy
You are holy, holy
Precious Lord reveal your heart to me
Father holy, holy

The universe declares your majesty
you are holy, holy, holy, holy

Halleluiah to the Lord of heaven and earth
Halleluiah to the Lord of heaven and earth
Halleluiah to the Lord of heaven and earth
Halleluiah to the Lord of heaven and earth
Halleluiah to the Lord of heaven and earth
Halleluiah to the Lord of heaven and earth

About The Author

Doug Gilmer is the Backcountry Chaplain™. A graduate of Liberty University, Doug went on to complete his studies at Luther Rice Seminary in Lithonia, GA, as well as a Masters  Photo by Bill Konway in Natural Resources (Wildlife Management and Recreation Design & Development) from Virginia Tech. Today, Doug combines his love for the outdoors, wildlife, hunting, and fishing, with his love for helping others. He provides spiritual care for members of the outdoor industry and outdoor media while also serving as a professor and the program director for the Adventure Leadership and Outdoor Ministry academic program at Liberty University. A military veteran and an active reservist, Doug is also passionate about assisting members of the armed forces who have been wounded in the line of duty and or are suffering from the effects of Post-Traumatic Stress and Traumatic Brain Injury by providing outdoor recreational therapy opportunities. Interestingly, although he has been a lifelong lover of the outdoors, his use of the outdoors as a ministry tool began during a 20+ year "tentmaker" ministry where he served in law enforcement and used this vocation to help fund and develop efforts to reach young people.

In between teaching, speaking, working with churches and outdoor organizations, Doug is a frequent contributor to a variety of outdoor magazines and outdoor media channels. He currently serves on the Board of Directors of the Professional Outdoor Media Association.

Doug and his family make their home in Virginia and he travels frequently between his home, northern Maine, Alaska, and other outdoor destinations around the country as he pursues the mission of the Backcountry Chaplain: leading lives lived outside"™.

Connect with Doug

E-mail: Doug@GilmerOutdoors.com
Twitter: @DouglasGilmer
Facebook: www.Facebook.com/BackcountryChaplain or www.Facebook.com/LU.ALOM
On the Web: www.BackcountryChaplain.com
www.GilmerOutdoors.com
www.Smoldering-Lake-Outfitters.com

Contact the publisher

Backcountry Adventures Press

www.backcountryadventurespress.com

darin@backcountryadventurespress.com

Notes

Made in the USA
Middletown, DE
21 August 2018